To the Midlothian Public Library, where I fell in love with books.

—LK

To my first library, the Richmondtown NYPL,
and all the hardworking librarians around the world.

—RS

World's
BEST
Librarian

• Published by Sourcebooks eXplore, an imprint of Sourcebooks Kids • P.O. Box 4410, Naperville, Illinois 60567-4410 • (630) 961-3900 • sourcebookskids.com • Cataloging-in-Publication Data is on file with the Library of Congress. • Source of Production: 1010 Printing Asia Limited, Kwun Tong, Hong Kong, China • Date of Production: February 2024 • Run Number: 5029804 • Printed and bound in China. • OGP 10 9 8 7 6 5 4 3 2 1

A Love Letter to My Library

Words by **Lisa Katzenberger**

New York Times bestselling illustrator **Rob Sayegh Jr.**

sourcebooks
eXplore

Activities

Story Time
3:00pm

Arts & Crafts
4:00pm

Open Every day
8am

Dear Library, thank you

for warm welcomes as I skip through your open doors.

Thank you, library,
for books in every nook and cranny.

Thank you, library,

for story time where I snuggle in a lap, cozy and warm.

Thank you, library,

for taking me on adventures from the seas to the stars.

Thank you, library,

for the little fish in the big tank who always looks like she's smiling.

Thank you, library,

for spaces and spots just the right size for me and a friend.

Thank you, library,

for smiles that turn into giggles that turn into loud laughs.

Thank you, library,

for little books made for little hands.

Thank you, library,

for crafts made with sticky glue and bright crayons and lots of love.

Thank you, library,

for connecting me to family that's far away.

Thank you, library,

for helpers who bring me stories with kids who look just like me.

Thank you, library,

for that quiet corner when I need a break.

Thank you, library,

for classes where I learn something new.

Thank you, library,

for letting me borrow the perfect book
that I hug hard the whole way home...

...until it is time to return again!
With love from all of us.

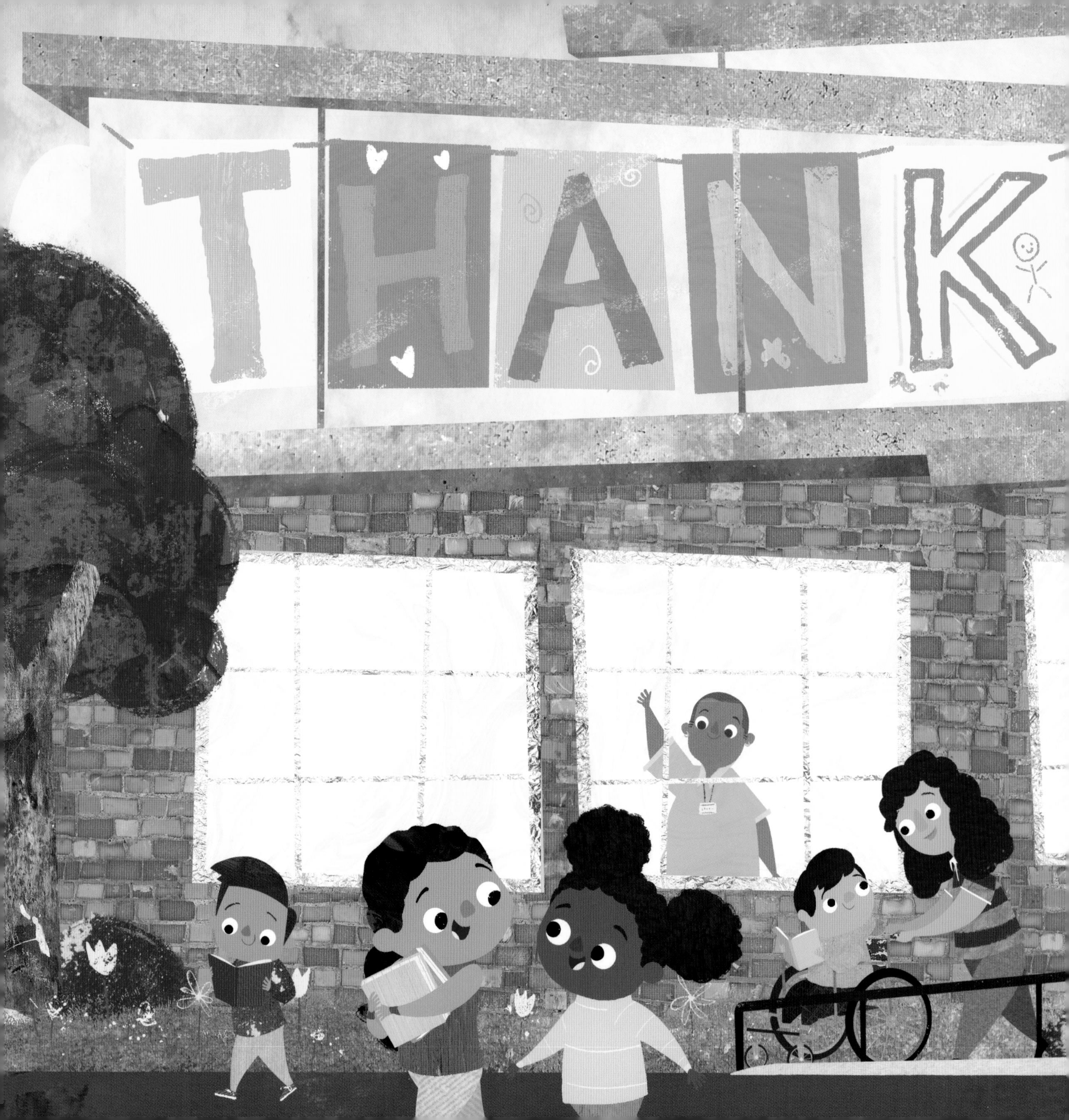
THANK

Y
U
LIBRARY
Activities
Story Time
3:00pm
Arts & Crafts
4:00pm
Open Every day
8am-6pm

Dear Library,

We ♥ You!

With love from all of us

Thank You!